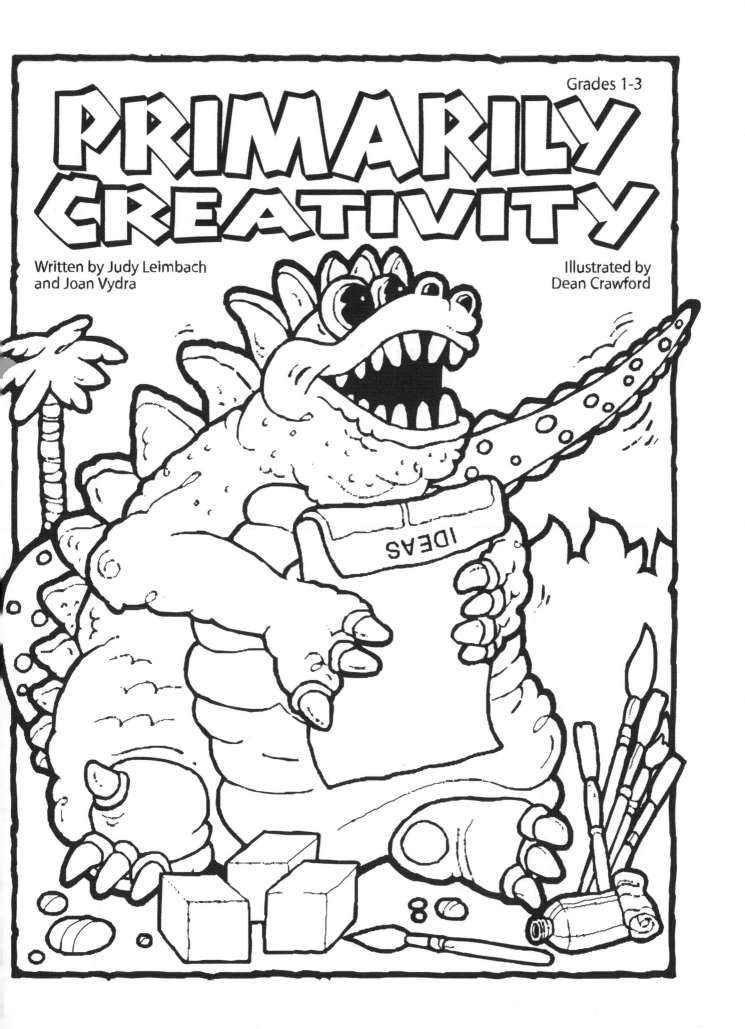

First published in 2005 by Prufrock Press Inc.

Published in 2021 by Routledge
605 Third Avenue, New York, NY 10017
2 Park Square, Milton Park, Abingdon, Oxon OX14 4RN

Routledge is an imprint of the Taylor & Francis Group, an informa business

Copyright © 2005 by Taylor & Francis Group

ISBN: 9781593630362 (pbk)

DOI: 10.4324/9781003237242

Contents

Introduction

Educators are faced with the awesome challenge of preparing students for what they might encounter in the future. Preparation for the future requires that children are prepared with more than the one-solution process, more than the right-answer, convergent thinking required by many learning activities in our classrooms. The kinds of problems people will face in the future will require differentiated thinking. We cannot teach children all of the right answers, because none of us even know the questions. We can, however, provide our students with the skills needed to tackle the many problems that they will face.

An emphasis on creative thinking skills in the classroom necessitates providing students with open-ended assignments and encouragement as they search for new answers. Unlike typical textbook questions that have a given right answer, creative questioning and thinking assumes that there may not be one right answer, but many possibilities.

Students will not think creatively unless they are confronted with challenging tasks in a supportive environment. Teachers need to recognize the importance of incorporating creative thinking into all areas of the curriculum. As students practice the many creative thinking tasks throughout this book, they will develop creative thinking skills, enabling them to become more capable and flexible learners, better prepared to handle future challenges.

Primarily Creativity is specifically designed to develop various kinds of creative thinking skills in primary children. The book is divided into eight areas. These eight areas of creative thinking are:
1. **Awareness** – The ability to notice characteristics of things in the environment so as to build a knowledge base that is the beginning of all other forms of creative thinking.
2. **Curiosity** – The ability and inclination to wonder about things and mentally explore the possibilities.
3. **Imagination** – The ability to speculate about things that are not necessarily based in reality.
4. **Fluency** – The ability to produce a large quantity of ideas.
5. **Flexibility** – The ability to look at things from several different perspectives or viewpoints; to pursue different angles of thinking.
6. **Originality** – The ability to produce new, novel, unique ideas.
7. **Elaboration** – The ability to add on to an idea; to give details, build groups of related ideas or expand on ideas.
8. **Perseverance** – The ability to keep trying to find an answer; to see a task through to completion.

Each section includes an explanation of the particular type of creative behavior, a list of questions, a list of tasks or activities that would require this behavior, and several reproducible worksheets.

DOI: 10.4324/9781003237242-1

Awareness

Awareness is the start of all creative thinking. Creativity does not occur in a vacuum. It must build on the knowledge that the learner has already acquired. The act of being aware necessitates paying attention to what is going on in the immediate environment and inside one's self. For example, awareness is knowing the streets in your neighborhood, knowing classroom rules, and knowing how it feels to step in squishy mud with your bare feet. Awareness is a wide range of experiences as well as the accumulation of data.

Children use their awareness in a variety of ways. For example, when children are asked to line up in alphabetical order according to first names, the learners must know the order of the alphabet, how we alphabetize, and also the correct spellings of the names of the other students in the class. When asked to find ways things are alike or different, children are assisted in the task by heightened awareness of attributes and characteristics. In the affective area, students' social/interpersonal skills are improved by an awareness of other people and their feelings and an ability to read nonverbal cues.

To help learners become aware, we must provide them with tasks that cause them to pay attention to and notice things in their surroundings.

The ability to notice the attributes of things in the environment so as to build a knowledge base that is the beginning of all other forms of creative thinking.

Questions to elicit awareness include:
1. How many _____?
2. What does _____ look like? Sound like? Taste like? Feel like?
3. Where is _____ usually found?
4. What are the attributes of a _____?
5. What does _____ have in common with ___?
6. How are _____ and _____ alike or different?
7. When (or how often) does _____ occur?
8. What is _____?
9. What are all the things that are ___?
10. What are the parts or features?

DOI: 10.4324/9781003237242-2

Awareness Tasks

1. How many consonants are in the alphabet?
2. How many days are in each month?
3. What is the exact title of your spelling book?
4. What are some of the ingredients of your favorite cereal?
5. How many people are in your classroom?
6. Does peanut butter need to be refrigerated?
7. Does jelly need to be refrigerated?
8. Where does ham come from?
9. What is your mother's maiden name?
10. How many windows are in your classroom?
11. What row of a typewriter keyboard contains the letter B?
12. How many sides does a plain gold school pencil have?
13. Which is larger, a penny or a dime?
14. How many sides does a stop sign have?
15. Which president's picture is on a penny? A nickel? A quarter?
16. Which president is pictured on a one-dollar bill?
17. How much does a first-class stamp cost?
18. What is the school secretary's name?
19. What is the name of the street in front of the school?
20. What does the silverware or dishes that your family uses look like?
21. How does it feel to walk through the grass?
22. What things are soft and furry?
21. Look at this ___. Close your eyes and picture it in your mind. Draw it.
22. Without looking, tell what your neighbor is wearing.
23. Listen to the music. Describe how it made you feel.
24. What else sounds like wood burning?
25. Go outside and select an object. Become that object for five minutes. Look at it, feel it, think about it. Explain what you experienced.
26. What words would you use to describe ___?

Creative thinkers are very observant. This means they really **look** at things in the world around them. Look around your classroom and see how observant you can be.

How many doors are there? _____

How many lights are there? _____

List all the round things you can see.

_____

_____

_____

_____

_____

List things in your classroom that have holes.

_____

_____

_____

_____

_____

Extra: On the back of this paper, draw a picture of something in your room you have never noticed before. Write three sentences about it.

Find a person in your classroom who has two sisters. Have that person write his or her name in the first box. Do the same for each of the other boxes on this page. Try to use a different person for each box.

1. Has two sisters	2. Loves soccer	3. Was born in another state
4. Has a cat	5. Hates spinach	6. Likes snakes
7. Takes piano lessons	8. Has a younger brother	9. Loves chocolate
10. Has a red bike	11. Is the youngest in the family	12. Knows at least five words in another language

At Home

How well do you know your own home? Do you really look at the things around you every day? Try to answer the questions below.   Then take this paper home and see if you were correct.

	Guess	Correct Answer

1. How many chairs are in your house? _____

2. What color are the walls in your kitchen? _____

3. How many stairs are inside your home? _____

4. How many electrical outlets are in your living room? _____

5. How many clocks do you have? _____

6. How many cupboard doors are in the kitchen? _____

7. What color is the outside of your front door? _____

8. Does your front door open out or in? _____

9. How many closets are in your house? _____

10. List at least three things in your home that you have never noticed before.

_____

_____

_____

_____

_____

Flags

Countries, states, and cities all have flags. Think about all the characteristics of a flag. Write words to describe everything you can think of about a flag.

_____

_____

_____

_____

_____

_____

_____

Now design your own flag for the Kingdom of Kids.

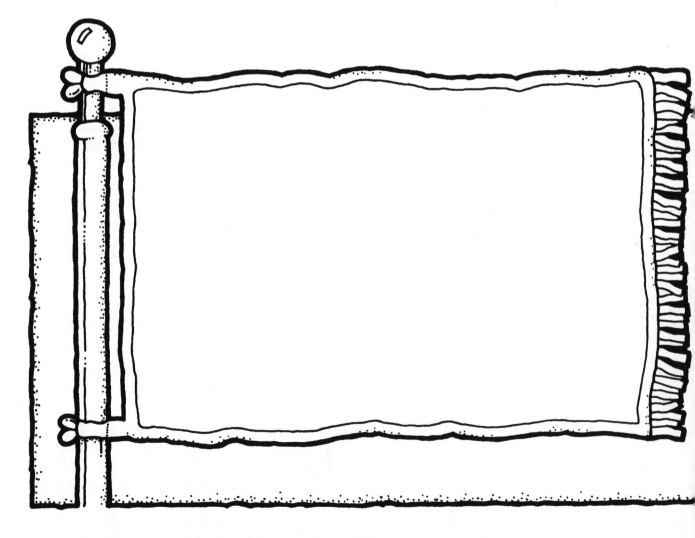

Curiosity

The ability and inclination to wonder about things and mentally explore the possibilities.

Curious thinking consists of wondering about or contemplating how or why things are, might be, or could be. The curious thinker mentally explores the possibilities that start from a basic fund of knowledge. For example, a curious child might wonder what holds the sky up in the air or makes the ocean blue. That same child might wonder why some men are bald and whether there is life on a still-unknown planet. Curious children constantly add the dimension of questioning to their search for new knowledge. Their research may raise as many new questions as it provides answers.

Another example of curious behavior is to wonder what might happen if the experiment is performed in a different way or if a given rule or principle is really true. Students might also wonder what would have happened if Columbus had sailed to a different location. Curious thinking generates interesting possibilities.

Teachers can help develop curiosity by asking students to be inquisitive about their learning. For example, in a science lesson, the teacher might ask questions along the line of, "What will happen if I add this to the solution?" In social studies, we might ask the learners to generate a list of questions that they would like to have answered.

We need students to continue to ask why and continue to search for possibilities all along the way. Students who are curious thinkers travel farther along the road toward becoming life-long learners and problem solvers.

Teachers encourage children to be curious learners when they provide strategies (not answers) for answering questions generated by curiosity and when they encourage students to ask questions as well as answer questions. Teachers who value curiosity might respond to a child's question with a reply of, "What an interesting question; how do you think you might find the answer?"

Other questions that would encourage curiosity include:
1. What might happen when___?
2. What would happen if we ___?
3. Why do you suppose ___ happened?
4. Why do you suppose ___ is true?
5. Image what ___ would be like.
6. What questions does this raise for you?
7. What else would you like to find out?
8. What do you wonder about?
9. What do you know? What do you not know?

DOI: 10.4324/9781003237242-3

Curiosity Tasks

1. If you didn't have to go to school, what would you do?
2. Why aren't there many mountains in the states beginning with the letter I?
3. What makes the sky seem blue?
4. How much is a million?
5. What would it be like to live on the other side of the world?
6. How would your life be different if you lived in Japan? Greece? Mexico?
7. What might be some different kinds of cereal someone who has no teeth could eat?
8. How does a camera work? How would you find out?
9. How are trees made into paper?
10. What things would you ask the main character in the book you are reading?
11. What things don't you know about our state?
12. How does the term bee-line relate to bees?
13. Where do numbers come from?
14. Where does the fog go?
15. What would it be like to be an astronaut?
16. Is there really an abominable snowman?
17. Why are there so many skyscrapers in New York?
18. Why does the Tower of Pisa lean?
19. What is the longest word in the dictionary?
20. Which utensil is used the most, knives, spoons or forks?
21. Why don't all people have the same color of hair and skin?
22. What would you like to ask an alien?
23. What do you **not** know about Jack and Jill?

Wondering

Everyone is curious about different things. People wonder about things that happened in the past. They wonder about things that are going on now that they don't understand. And they wonder about what will happen in the future. Curious people ask a lot of *how* and *why* questions. What are some things you wonder about?

Past

I wonder _____

I wonder _____

I wonder _____

Present

I wonder _____

I wonder _____

I wonder _____

Future

I wonder _____

I wonder _____

I wonder _____

Extra: Do you think you could find the answers to any of the questions on this page? Think about how you would find the answers.

When you are curious about something, what do you do? Check all of the statements that fit you.

___ I wonder about it a lot.

___ I try to figure it out by myself.

___ I ask other people questions about it.

___ I look in the encyclopedia.

___ I try to find a book about it.

___ I just forget about it.

___ I ask my parents or teacher.

___ I experiment.

Curiosity is a wonderful thing. It keeps us thinking and learning. We feel good when we can find answers to our questions.

Here are some curious questions about animals. See how many of the answers you can find.

1. Do porcupines really shoot their quills? _____

2. Are bats blind? _____

3. Why do raccoons wash their food? _____

_____

4. Do bulls get angry and charge when they see red? _____

5. Are elephants afraid of mice? _____

6. Why do sharks keep moving all the time? _____

_____

7. Are elephants the largest living animals? _____

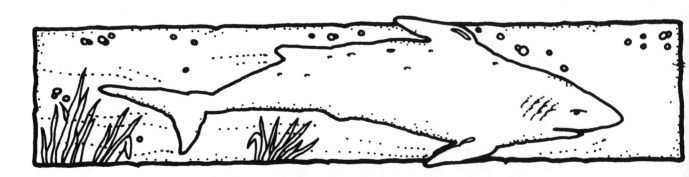

Asking Questions

Curious thinkers have lots of questions. Thinking up good questions can be just as much fun as finding the answers. Think about outer space and about nature. What else would you like to know about either subject? Write *who, why, what, where* and *how* questions about outer space and nature.

Outer Space	Nature
Who _____	Who _____
_____	_____
_____	_____
Why _____	Why _____
_____	_____
_____	_____
What _____	What _____
_____	_____
_____	_____
Where _____	Where _____
_____	_____
_____	_____
How _____	How _____
_____	_____
_____	_____

Imagination

Imaginative behavior is pondering the many "what if's" in life. Students using their imaginations can consider things that are not necessarily possible, while curious thinking is generated from real possibilities. Imagination is speculating about things unknown or thinking about what might be possible. For example, an imaginative learner might ask the question, "How might things be different if people walked on four legs like dogs?"

The purpose of imagination is to develop the ability to visualize images of unknowns, to imagine about people, places, and things that might not exist or to break away from accepted answers or trains of thought. Imagination is a creative thinking skill because it characterizes the learner who dares to think and wonder beyond the known or usual parameters.

The ability to speculate about things that are not necessarily based in reality.

Imagination occurs within the regular school content when students wonder about ways things might be different. For example, what might happen if words were spelled the way they sound to each speller or what might happen if there were no accepted standards for counting and measuring?

Imagination gives rise to ideas for creative writing assignments, unique insights into literature selections, and applications or extensions of scientific principles. Imagination lets us look at not only what does exist or did happen, but also what might have been or what might be possible.

Students with vivid imaginations disregard the usual limitations and what really exists. They approach things with a fresh, unrestrained outlook. This ability to imagine correlates with the ability to produce original thoughts and products. It is a particularly useful skill when students are able to apply imaginative thinking to a real-life situation in order to generate new and original perspectives, understandings, and solutions.

A teacher encourages imaginative thinking when he or she provides opportunities for stretching beyond our known world and guarantees a safe environment for the kind of risk-taking demonstrated by the imaginative thinker.

Questions to encourage imaginative thinking would include:
1. What would you do if ___?
2. Imagine ___. What would it be like?
3. If you could ___(do something), what would you do?
4. You have been given the power to ___. How will you use it?
5. What if ___?
6. Suppose ___. How would things be different?
7. What would happen if?

DOI: 10.4324/9781003237242-4

Imagination Tasks

1. What if ice cream cones grew on trees?
2. What if insects were as large as dogs?
3. What if the moon was really made of cheese?
4. What if people couldn't walk, but could only run?
5. What if it snowed every year on the Fourth of July?
6. How would it feel to be a letter lost in the mail?
7. What if rabbits were ferocious?
8. What would happen if birthday cake tasted like mud?
9. What if horses could talk to humans?
10. What would happen if the Atlantic Ocean dried up?
11. What would it be like if people hibernated like bears?
12. Take a mind trip to Never Never Land. Tell what you saw.
13. Be a feather and describe your best adventure.
14. If you had magic powers, how could you use them to make the world a better place?
15. If you were making the book you are reading into a movie, what special effects would you use to make it more interesting?
16. How could a magical unicorn solve the problem of ___?
17. What if people could only smile (and not frown)?
18. Make a drawing that shows "sparkling."
19. Be a person with special powers and tell how you would help the characters in the book you are reading.
20. Take a Popcorn Express to the Land of Peanut Butter and Jelly. What would you see, hear, smell, and do?
21. What might a sneeg look like? What would it eat?
22. Pretend you could catch a falling star. What would you do with it?

The song *Somewhere Over the Rainbow* describes what things are like on the other side of the rainbow. Have you ever thought about a land on the other side of the rainbow?

Close your eyes and imagine what it would be like at the end of the rainbow. Then open your eyes and draw a picture of the imaginary land you saw with your mind's eye.

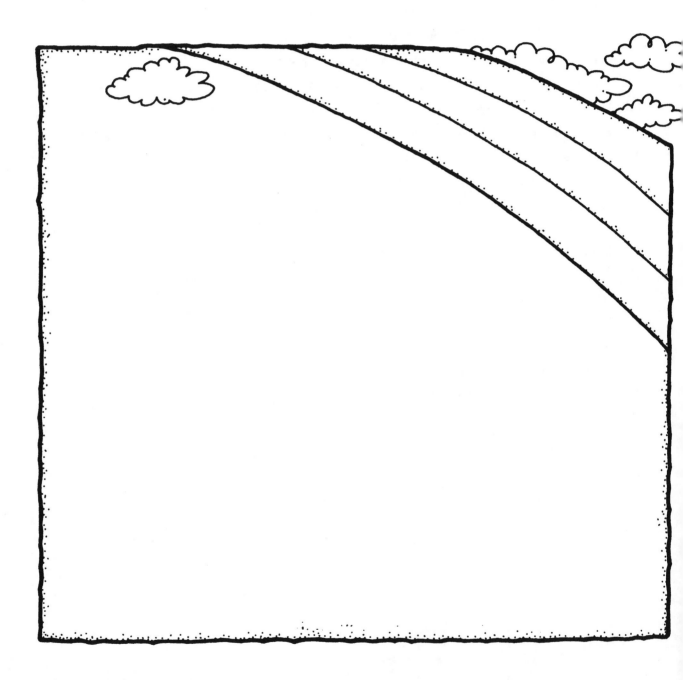

Extra: Describe what wonderful adventures await children in this land.

What If . . . ?

Dragons and unicorns are mythological creatures that have captured our imagination. Use **your** imagination to think of what it would be like if one of these creatures was real rather than make-believe. Imagine that you had one of the animals for a pet.

Draw a picture of your pet.

List some of the things you could do with this unusual pet.

1. _____
2. _____
3. _____
4. _____
5. _____

Extra: Use your ideas to write a story called "My Wonderful, Unusual Pet."

In the poem "If I Were in Charge of the World," the author tells what changes she would make. For example, in her world, she would:
- cancel Monday mornings
- have brighter night lights
- not have lonely or clean
- have chocolate sundaes with whipped cream and nuts be vegetables.

Imagine **you** are in charge of the world. What changes will you make?

_____

_____

_____

_____

_____

_____

_____

_____

_____

_____

_____

_____

_____

_____

_____

_____

_____

Note to teachers: Poem from the book *If I Were in Charge of the World* by Judith Viorst, Antheneum, New York.

Picturing Changes

We are used to having two arms, two legs, two hands, and two feet.
We usually take our hands, feet, fingers, and toes for granted.

Choose one change from each list and illustrate them to show how you
would look if:

Your hands...
- had fingers 10 inches long
- had eyes on the end of the thumbs
- were shaped like balloons

Your feet...
- were webbed
- were two feet thick
- were two feet long

Extra: On a different piece of paper, write a story that tells how your life would be
different if you really looked like this.

Fluency

Fluent thinking is the mental flow of ideas and thoughts. It is the ability to produce a large quantity of creative ideas. Fluency activities may ask the learner to generate answers to questions of how many, what kinds, or what else. Fluent thinkers produce lots of ideas.

Fluency tasks cause a search through the learner's private collection or storehouse of knowledge and experiences for all possible responses. For example, brainstorming in small groups promotes fluency, as one person's idea triggers more responses from other members of the group. It's important in fluent thinking exercises to withhold all judgments of right or wrong, appropriate or inappropriate, because the attention is placed on quantity rather than the quality of the responses. This allows for an uninterrupted flow of thoughts and ideas and a search for all possibilities. The rationalization for promoting fluent thinking is that the more responses that are produced, the greater are the odds of producing an original idea or of producing a satisfactory solution. If you have twenty ideas to choose from, you have a greater probability of having a quality idea within that group than if you have only two ideas.

The ability to produce a large quantity of ideas.

A teacher encourages fluent thinking every time he or she asks:
1. How many ___ can you think of?
2. In what ways might we ___?
3. What are all the ways you could ___?
4. Make a long list of things that ___ .
5. How many different examples (reasons, solutions, etc.) can you think of?
6. How many ways can you think of to ___?
7. What are all the things that are ___?
8. What comes to mind when you think of ___?
9. How long a list can you make?

DOI: 10.4324/9781003237242-5

22

Fluency Tasks

Make a long list of:
- scary sounds
- metal things found in a school
- types of hats
- things you do with a clothespin
- things that are orange and round
- things to do in a haunted house
- things that are huge and soft
- red things found in a grocery store
- things that have to do with the sun
- uses for a single wheel
- things to do with old magazines
- things with dots
- round things smaller than a basketball
- round things larger than a basketball
- things that are warm
- things that make crunchy sounds
- things that can be cold
- ways to be kind to someone
- words that make you think of fun
- everything that comes to mind when you think of 100
- ways to catch an idea
- titles for a book about chocolate
- uses for an old tire
- things that mean love
- uses for a sea shell
- uses for a pile of cardboard
- ways to make spelling fun
- ways to save energy
- all the things that sparkle
- all the things that can be ___ .
- things that make the sound "hiss"
- sounds related to water
- things that are invisible
- ways to lift a heavy object
- ways to pop a balloon

This page will give you practice in making lists. Make one list of the things you will do today. Make one list of the things you would like to do today. List as many things as you can.

Things I will do today

Things I would like to do today

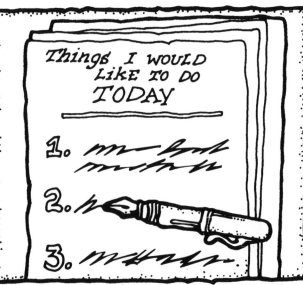

Write at least four words that rhyme with each of these words.

hat   cry   big

_____   _____   _____

_____   _____   _____

_____   _____   _____

_____   _____   _____

_____   _____   _____

_____   _____   _____

gate   bed   hug

_____   _____   _____

_____   _____   _____

_____   _____   _____

_____   _____   _____

_____   _____   _____

_____   _____   _____

Brainstorming

Brainstorming is thinking of a lot of ideas. Your teacher will give you a topic to brainstorm. Make a long list of ideas. Do not judge whether the ideas are good or bad. Just write as many ideas as possible.

How many _____ can you think of?

_____

_____

_____

_____

_____

_____

_____

_____

_____

_____

_____

_____

_____

_____

_____

_____

_____

_____

Extra: After you have thought of a lot of ideas, put a ∗ by the three best ideas.

How many different things can you make out of the shapes below? Try to make something different out of each one. You can turn the page any way you like.

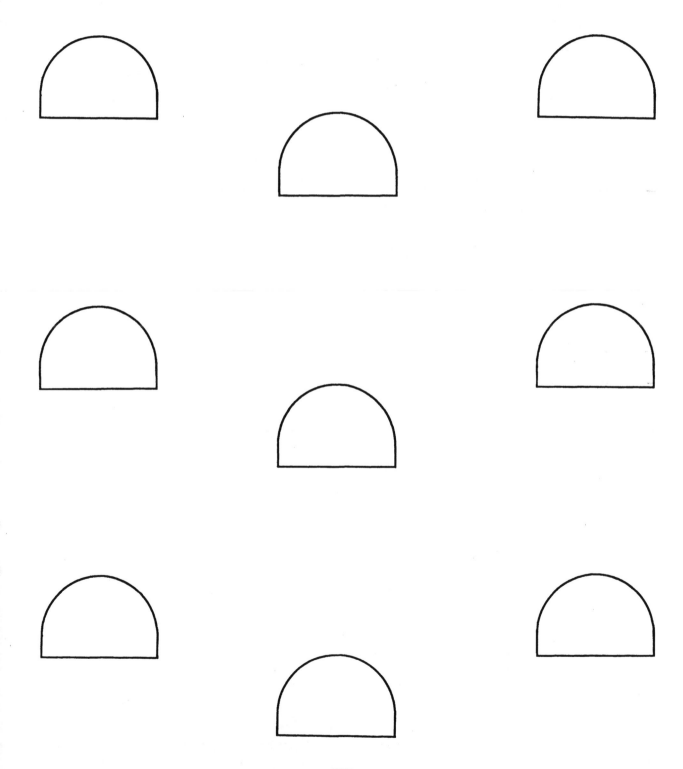

Reasoning Why

Johnny sat at his desk but didn't read his book. Some reasons for this might be:

- Johnny didn't know how to read.
- Johnny couldn't find his book.
- Johnny didn't have his glasses.
- Johnny was supposed to be listening, not reading.
- It was time for math, not reading.

For each situation listed below, give at least five good reasons why this might be happening.

The little boy sat on the steps crying.

_____

_____

_____

_____

_____

The grass is wet.

_____

_____

_____

_____

_____

Reasoning Why

For each situation listed below, give at least five good reasons why this might be happening.

Sarah didn't go to school today.

_____

_____

_____

_____

_____

_____

_____

Your mother is baking a cake.

_____

_____

_____

_____

_____

_____

_____

When we have a problem we have to think of things we might do to solve our problem. The more ideas we can think of, the better chance we have of solving the problem. Look at these two problems and think of some of the things you might do in each situation.

I forgot my lunch.

Things I could do:

I want a toy that costs $3.00 and I only have $1.00.

Things I could do:

_____
_____
_____
_____
_____
_____
_____
_____
_____

_____
_____
_____
_____
_____
_____
_____
_____
_____

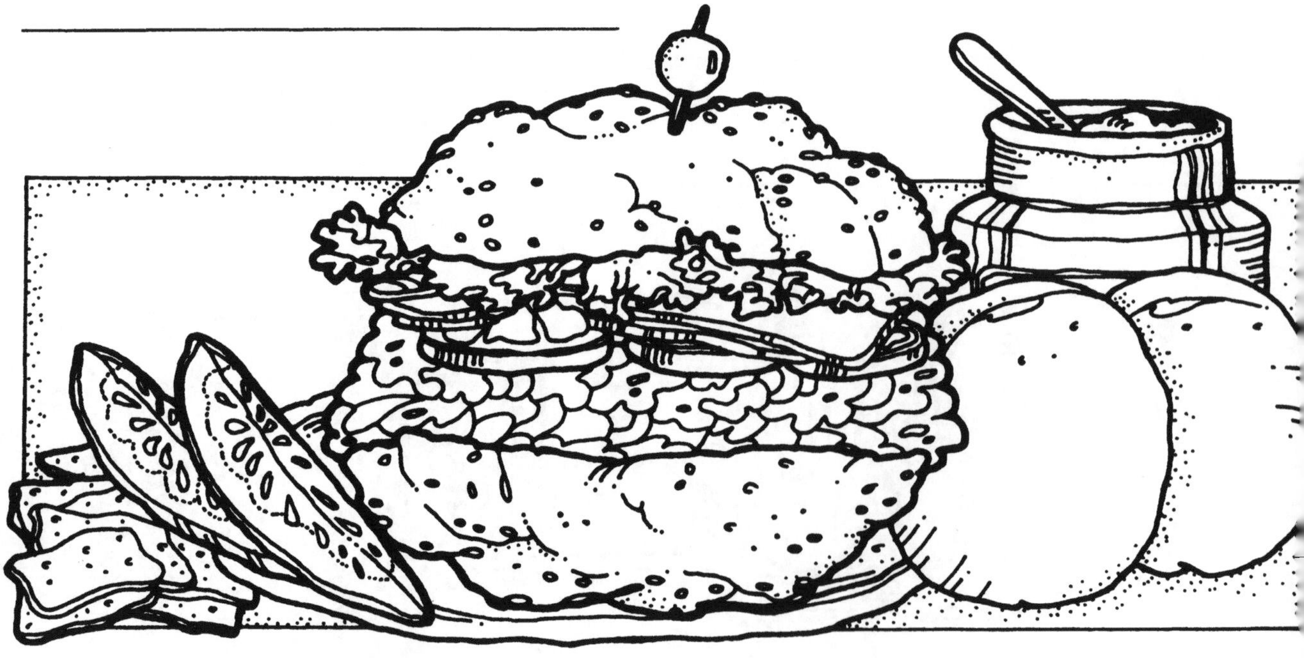

Everyone has problems. Some of them are little problems and some are big problems. See how many ideas you can think of for either a problem your teacher gives you or for one of your own problems. Make a long list of possible ideas.

The problem is _____

_____

Things I might do are:

_____

_____

_____

_____

_____

_____

_____

_____

_____

_____

_____

_____

_____

_____

Flexibility

Flexible thinking extends fluent thinking. Flexibility results in many different kinds of ideas. It is the ability to look at things from different angles, see the situation from several perspectives. It is the ability to shift trains of thought and produce a variety of ideas. The flexible thinker produces original ideas by forcing associations not usually thought of in a given context. A student who thinks flexibly often redefines mental sets by viewing things from other perspectives. The flexible thinker responds well to the question, "What else is possible?"

The ability to look at things from several different perspectives or viewpoints; to pursue different angles of thinking.

If asked in what ways an empty paper towel tube could be used, a flexible response might be to use it as a measure for spaghetti or as a tunnel for ants. When asked what one dangling earring could be used for, the learner might suggest using it as a chandelier in a doll house or as a fishing lure. The flexible thinker will be able to produce a variety of ideas. From this ability to see things from many different angles comes the ability to produce a larger quantity of ideas (fluency) and more unique ideas (originality).

The purpose of flexible thinking is to generate and promote responses that deviate from the normal thought patterns. Flexibility allows for invention and the discovery of new or untested ideas. Flexible thinkers see things in different ways and can find uses for almost anything. This shift in direction and perspective comes through the breaking of mindsets, the brave world of the flexible thinker.

Children become flexible thinkers whenever a teacher asks:
1. Can you think of a different way to ___?
2. What else might be happening?
3. What other things are possible?
4. What are all of the possibilities?
5. What are some different ways to look at this?
6. How would ___ look at this?
7. What are some different reasons for ___?
8. What if ___?
9. What ideas can you get about ___ by thinking about ___?
10. ___ is to ___ as ___ is to ___. (analogy)
11. What else could you use ___ for?
12. In what ways are ___ and ___ alike?
13. What relationship can you think of between ___ and ___?

DOI: 10.4324/9781003237242-6

Flexibility Tasks

1. How could you find the width or length of your classroom without using a ruler or yardstick?

2. How could you cook dinner without a stove, oven, or microwave?

3. Think of one way to use a blanket other than as a cover.

4. Think of one way to open a car door without touching it.

5. Think of at least five ways to use an empty box (besides the idea of holding something).

6. Find three ways that these words are alike:

   little   giant   light

7. Write five sentences using the word "read" in different ways.

8. Write four different sentences that show anger.

9. Draw three things you can do with an old gym shoe.

10. Think of two sentences you could write without using any words. Example: ICAB.

11. Think of new uses for pencils other than writing.

12. Make a shape that is strong.

13. Find several different ways to show the idea of confusion.

14. What is the color of love? The smell of fun? The sound of soft?

15. How might these people view playground balls differently: children, the custodian, the principal, the neighbors?

16. How can you catch a flying insect without using a net?

17. What might be some reasons for not wearing shoes?

18. If you were an ant, what would small mean to you?

19. Which is softer, yellow or a feather?

20. How many different words fit into this sentence:

    Money is the ___ of ___ .

    Music is ___ to ___ .

21. How could you use the idea of a pizza to solve the problem of a noisy classroom?

22. How is a pencil like a plant?

23. In what ways is magic like a feather?

24. How is a teacup like a telephone?

25. Describe a ___ as seen by a ___ .

26. If you were a ball, what would recess mean to you?

27. Describe your mood as a weather forecast.

Other Uses

Be a creative thinker. Think of other uses for these ordinary objects.

Pencils are usually used for writing. Think of several other things you could do with a pencil besides using it for writing.

_____

_____

_____

_____

Soup cans hold soup. Think of several uses for a soup can besides being used as a container.

_____

_____

_____

_____

Gum is for chewing. Think of several other uses for gum.

_____

_____

_____

_____

Most children get to school by walking, riding a bus or being driven in a car. Think of several other ways a child could get to school.

_____

_____

_____

_____

_____

_____

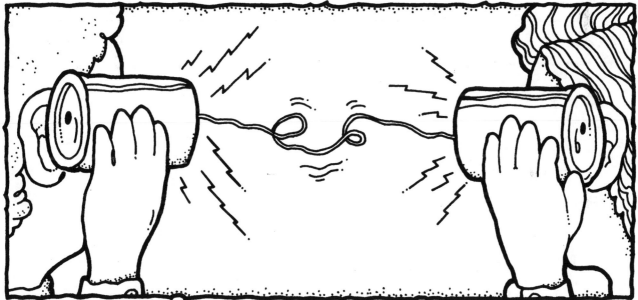

If you wanted to give your friend a message you could call him or her on the telephone. Think of several other ways you could get a message to your friend.

_____

_____

_____

_____

_____

Many words have more than one meaning. Think of the different meanings of the words below and write sentences using each word in three different ways.

Spring

1. _____

_____

_____

Hand

2. _____

_____

_____

Run

3. _____

_____

_____

Combinations

Write five different sentences. Use at least one word from each list in every sentence. Cross out the words as you use them so no word is used more than once. You may add other words to the sentences to make them sound right.

A	B	C
mailman	can	cat
kangaroo	match	rug
ribbon	bat	table
child	park	statue
school	light	newspaper
heart	watch	pipe
mouse	skipped	saucer

1. _____
_____

2. _____
_____

3. _____
_____

4. _____
_____

5. _____
_____

There were two outs in the last inning. I was up to bat with one person on base. Our team was behind by one run. It was up to me. The pitcher wound up. The ball came sailing toward the plate. "I'm going to kill it," I thought. "I'll knock it out of here!" I swung as hard as I could, and sure enough, I hit the ball clear over the fence. I was a hero!

Rewrite this paragraph from the viewpoint of the ball.

_____

_____

_____

_____

_____

_____

_____

_____

_____

_____

_____

_____

I was ready to go to school when I noticed that it was raining. I love walking in the rain, so I quickly got on my raincoat and boots, grabbed my umbrella out of the closet, and raced out the door. As I splashed down the street, I listened to the rain beating against my umbrella. Now and then the wind would blow some rain drops into my face. I happily waded through every puddle between my house and school. Even when I got to school, I stayed out in the rain for awhile and enjoyed breathing the clean, fresh air.

This paragraph describes walking in the rain from a person's point of view. Write a paragraph describing a rainy day from an umbrella's point of view.

_____

_____

_____

_____

_____

_____

_____

_____

_____

_____

_____

_____

_____

_____

_____

Many Possibilities

List all the describing words you can think of that could fit in the blank to describe a dog.

The _____ dog

Think of words that describe size, age, breed, looks, or personality.

_____

_____

_____

_____

_____

_____

_____

_____

_____

_____

_____

_____

_____

_____

_____

_____

Extra: On another piece of paper, write all the words you can think of to describe a man. Try to think of many different things about a man to describe.

Providing Questions

If the answer is **2**, what might the question be?

There are many questions that have the answer of 2. See how quickly you can think of different questions that have the answer "2" for each category below.

Math facts	Body parts
What is 6 – 4?	How many eyes do you have?

Things that come in twos	Letters or digits
How many mittens in a pair?	How many t's in little?

More Possibilities

If the answer is 5, what might the question be?
See how many different questions you can think of that could be answered "5." Think of many different categories.

_____

_____

_____

_____

_____

Did you think of questions about money, time, math facts, fingers and toes, number of letters in words or digits in a numeral?

The answer is "blue." What is the question?

_____

_____

_____

_____

_____

Drawing Ideas

You could use all of the shapes below to draw pictures of different animals, but that would not be very creative. A creative thinker likes to think of a variety of things. Make something different out of each oval. You may turn the page in any direction.

animal	person	plant
space vehicle	land vehicle	water vehicle
shelter	weather	your choice

Originality

The ability to produce new, novel, unique ideas.

Originality is the creative thinking behavior that produces new or novel responses. Originality is often the by-product of other creative thinking behaviors. For example, when working through a fluency exercise, some learners will produce ideas not thought of by anyone else. The more ideas that are produced (fluency), the better are the chances that there will be original responses. In a flexibility exercise, some learners will produce novel ideas as a result of thinking in different ways from other learners. These unique responses are examples of originality.

The most original idea can be the first generated or it can be the one that comes when learners are pushed for one more response. Original responses might come in tandem with fluent thinking, elaboration, flexibility, or perseverance; or possibly in a combination with several creative thinking processes. The more teachers stress creativity and divergent thinking, the greater the likelihood of original responses. Students will learn to value original thinking when teachers provide activities that facilitate original responses and also accept and recognize original thinking. Since original ideas may be distinct departures from the norms, the instructor must blend tolerance and open-mindedness with the ability to evaluate whether the idea not only stands out from the ordinary, but also meets the stated criteria.

A teacher can encourage students to be original by asking, "What else, or what more?" These questions, designed to promote fluent thinking, let students know that we want them to stretch their minds even more. Originality will happen in most classrooms where teachers provide daily experiences in fluent and flexible thinking.

Other questions and statements to elicit original thinking include:
1. What is a new, original way to ___?
2. How could you make it different?
3. What can you think of that no one else will think of?
4. Can you invent a new ___?
5. How can you change ___ to make ___?
6. How can you combine ___ and ___ to make something new?
7. How can you use ___ and ___ to solve the problem of ___?
8. Devise a new way to ___.
9. Create an ideal ___ for a ___.

DOI: 10.4324/9781003237242-7

Originality Tasks

1. Design a puzzle or a maze for a friend to solve.
2. Design your own secret code.
3. Create new words for a song you know.
4. Paint a picture of something from your imagination.
5. Create a new holiday to celebrate something special.
6. Describe a new animal that might become a household pet.
7. Create a conversation between sweet and sour.
8. Create an original simile for " as easy as . . ."
9. Invent a new game using two tennis rackets, a Nerf ball and a handball court.
10. Write a poem about ___ .
11. Write your own original definitions for these nonsense words.

    The boy *squzzled* the teddy bear.

    Squzzle means to _____ .
12. Design a hat that would also serve as a purse.
13. Create original traffic signs for skateboarding.
14. Create your own recipe for happiness.
15. Give students cartoons and have them write their own captions.
16. Invent a new kind of ice cream. Give it a name.
17. Invent a new name for pencils that have been chewed by their owners.
18. Write an owner's manual for your math book.
19. Design a new, unusual way to show friendship.
20. Design a unique private place the main character in this story would like.
21. Design an original award for someone who is ___ .
22. Create a remedy for meanness.
23. Design a map that shows the way to healthy living.
24. Create something that expresses your uniqueness.

Being Different

An original idea is one that is unusual. It is different; not what most people would think of. Fill in the blanks with an **original** answer, something other than the usual answer that people your age would normally give.

1. The egg cracked and out came _____
   (not a chick or any kind of a bird)

2. The diver found a treasure chest at the bottom of the sea. When he opened it, he found _____
   (not silver, gold or jewels)

3. When the little boy pulled the cork out of the dusty old bottle, out came _____
   (not a genie)

4. The Easter Bunny left a basket filled with _____
   (not candy or eggs)

5. When Mrs. Jones looked out on the playground, she saw _____
   _____
   (not playground equipment or children)

Extra: Choose one of your original ideas and write a story about it on another piece of paper.

My Own Design

Every year, the Post Office issues commemorative stamps. These stamps commemorate a special event or honor a person or group of people. The first commemorative stamps were issued in 1893 honoring Columbus's discovery of America.

Think of a special event that you would like to commemorate or a group of people who you would like to honor and design a stamp for this occasion or for these people.

My Own Cereal

Invent a new cereal.

What are the main ingredients? _____

_____

What color (or colors) will it be? _____

Draw the shape or shapes of the pieces of cereal.

List six words to describe the cereal.

_____

_____

_____

What will the cereal be called?

_____

Design a box for your cereal.

Extra: On another piece of paper, write an advertising slogan or jingle that will make people want to buy your cereal.

Design a maze. Draw a character in the start box. In the finish box, draw something your character would want to reach. Draw all the lines to complete the maze. Use a ruler if you are using straight lines.

Start

Finish

C is for creativity. Think of an original idea for something you can make out of the C on this page. You may turn the page any direction you wish. Try to think of an idea that is different from anyone else's idea.

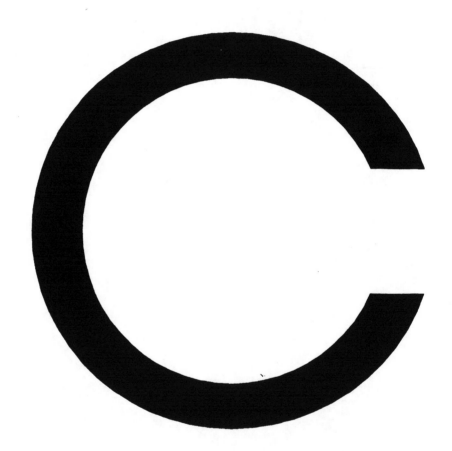

Extra: On another piece of paper, make a picture using your initials.

Drawing Ideas

How many things can you think of that you can make out of the lines below? Be original. Try to think of things that no one else will think of.

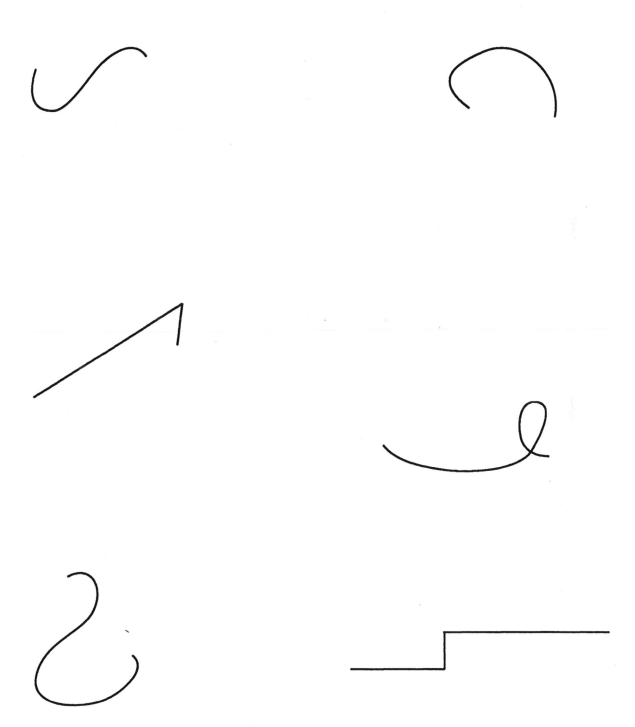

Elaboration

Elaboration is the creative thinking behavior that results in adding to or embellishing an idea. It is the ability to add details, fill in the gaps, build groups of related ideas and expand ideas. By adding onto a drawing, a sentence, a thought, or a story, the learner is making it a more complete, more interesting finished product. The purpose of elaboration is to expand or stretch; to add to our existing knowledge or the original idea.

Elaboration is a creative thinking skill because the learner is required to ask more questions and seek more answers than are generally given, or to take a simple idea and develop a more complex thought. Students elaborate when they change a simple sentence like "The dog ran " to a more complex sentence like "The mangy brown dog ran quickly away from the mischievous group of young boys." It is also elaboration (and originality) when a simple doodle is made from letters or lines. The more the learner elaborates on the original drawing, the more complex and creative the doodle becomes.

The ability to add on to an idea; to give details, build groups of related ideas or expand on ideas.

A teacher has children elaborate every time he or she asks a question like:
1. What else can you tell me about ___?
2. What can you add to make it more interesting/ complete?
3. Using these guidelines, what can you develop?
4. Using these basic elements, what can you create?
5. How can you complete this?
6. What could be added to ___ to make a new ___?
7. What new ideas can you add?

DOI: 10.4324/9781003237242-8

Elaboration Tasks

1. Illustrate an idiom like, "It's raining cats and dogs."
2. Paste a picture in the middle of a piece of paper. Use other art media to add details. Describe the result.
3. Pick a letter with a tail. Make the tail longer and create an interesting design with the letter.
4. Take a small piece of scrap paper and add details to make it into something interesting.
5. Make a thumbprint of your thumb using an ink pad. Add details to make it into something else.
6. Add words to sentences to make them more interesting.
7. Print your first, last, and middle names. Add details to make them into an interesting design.
8. Make a thought web about ___. Write down everything that is related to ___.
9. Finish the story that begins . . .
10. Create a game using a tennis racket, a jump rope, and a sock.
11. Complete this sentence, "Wishes, like butterflies, ___"
12. What would you do to make our school more beautiful?
13. Plan a party with a dinosaur theme.
14. Using the basic format of a cinquain (or some other form), create your own poem about summer.
15. Use the three letters "e-a-t" to make new words. You may add letters before, between, or after the letters.
16. Add details to make this shape into something else.
17. Draw a long straight line. Add details to make it into something.
18. Given an outline of a skyline of a city, draw in the individual buildings and features.
19. Given a basic cookie recipe, what could be added to make your own special cookies?
20. What can be added to a plain skateboard to make it more attractive to people your age?
21. What example can you think of that shows "A stitch in time saves nine"?
22. Write a story problem to show 30 + 20 = 50.
23. Describe what a television program called "All of Us Together" might be like.
24. Write a news article with a headline "Children Look Into the Future."
25. What can you add to a cardboard box to make a toy for a 4-year old?

Add your own ideas to this picture. Show what is growing on the tree, what is near the tree, what is in the tree, what is under the ground, and what is in the sky.

Descriptive Writing

Adding descriptive words and phrases can make a simple sentence much more interesting. Here's an example.

The clown danced.

The *funny little* clown danced.

The *funny little* clown *happily* danced *in circles around the circus tent*.

Add some descriptive words and phrases to each sentence.

1. The dog barked.

The _____ dog _____ barked

_____

2. The baby cried.

The _____ baby _____ cried

_____

3. The volcano erupted.

The _____ volcano _____ erupted

_____

4. The car sped.

The _____ car _____ sped

_____

5. The snow fell.

The _____ snow _____ fell

_____

Drawing Ideas

Draw a picture using all of the lines on this page. You may turn the paper any way you wish. Add details to your drawing and give it a title.

Write interesting, descriptive endings for the sentences below.

1. Joy is the color of _____

2. Being myself is _____

3. I feel important when _____

4. To be first is _____

5. If only _____

6. When I am 30 years old, I'll _____

7. Mud makes me _____

8. Being alone makes me _____

9. I am angriest when _____

10. I feel happy when _____

A man walked through the woods one day. He heard a noise in the bushes. He walked over to see what it was. He backed away. Then he ran.

This story is not very interesting. Add words and phrases on the blanks below to make the story more complete and fun to read.

A _____ man walked _____ through the

_____ woods one _____ day. He

_____ heard a _____ noise in the

_____ bushes. He walked _____ over

to see what it was. _____ he backed away.

Then he ran _____

because _____

_____

_____

Extra: Draw a picture of what he saw.
Think of at least five different titles for your story.

Perseverance

Perseverance is the creative thinking behavior of seeing a task through to the end, or at least to some satisfactory conclusion. It is avoiding the use of the word "can't," and replacing it with a sentence like "I haven't solved this yet, but I will do it!" Perseverance addresses the task commitment of the learner, the willingness to try other possibilities, and the need for goal completion without giving up or settling for less than the learner's best effort. Perseverance encourages a positive attitude toward problem solving. When one attempt fails, the persevering student tries another, and another, and another.

The ability to keep trying to find an answer; to see a task through to completion.

Teachers deal with the perseverance issue when students ask if a product is good enough or how long the story needs to be. The teacher can help nurture perseverance by turning the responsibility over to the learner. This might be done by answering queries with questions like:
"Are you satisfied with it?"
"What else can you do to make it better?"
"Would you change it in any way?"

Perseverance will come into play at different times for different learners. What requires perseverance for completion for one student might be easily solved by another student. Perseverance should not be busy work. Perseverance means quality time and effort needed for worthwhile task completion.

Teachers help develop perseverance whenever they encourage individual effort and provide responses like "I knew you could do it!" at the successful completion of a difficult task. Questions and statements that spur perseverance include:
1. How will you know when you are done?
2. What else can you do?
3. How else can you solve the problem?
4. You can do it with just a little more effort.

Perseverance Tasks

1. Solving a difficult jigsaw puzzle.
2. Unscrambling lists of words.
3. Solving difficult math problems.
4. Finding answers to riddles.
5. Finding facts not in the textbook.
6. Going back and writing a new ending to a story.
7. Working through a complicated maze.
8. Solving logic problems.

DOI: 10.4324/9781003237242-9

Animal Unscramble

Perseverance requires that you keep working on a task until it is done. Show your ability to persevere by unscrambling these familiar animal names. Don't give up until you have finished.

1. tac _____
2. serho _____
3. kduc _____
4. kendyo _____
5. fefairg _____
6. barbit _____
7. atgo _____
8. ykonme _____
9. hlewa _____
10. ktruey _____
11. karhs _____
12. pdhilon ∗ _____
13. dlolimaar ∗ _____
14. eeltpahn ∗ _____
15. hnoosurrice ∗ _____
16. pppaohtaimsu ∗ _____

∗ Bonus problems for persevering people.

Vocabulary

Each problem below has two letters. Using the first letter as the beginning of a word and the last letter as the end of a word, think of as many words as you can that fit each pattern. Don't give up until you have at least five words for each set of letters.

For example: H – E might be: *have, hole, here, hale, hike, hope, home, hire, huge, headache, or heave.*

S – R   P – L   B – K   C – E

_____   _____   _____   _____

_____   _____   _____   _____

_____   _____   _____   _____

_____   _____   _____   _____

_____   _____   _____   _____

_____   _____   _____   _____

B – Y   S – N   T – N   F – T

_____   _____   _____   _____

_____   _____   _____   _____

_____   _____   _____   _____

_____   _____   _____   _____

_____   _____   _____   _____

_____   _____   _____   _____

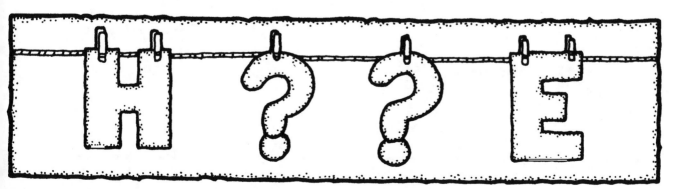

Problem Solving

Try solving these problems and then share the way you solved the problem with the other students in your class.

1. The land of Zoobrok has only creatures with three legs (Ooglies) and four legs (Moozos). These creatures are so tall that human visitors can only see their feet. When Bobby visited the Land of Zoobrok, he counted 31 feet. How many Ooglies and Moozos did Bobby meet? (Is there more that one right answer?)

2. Joan and Judy were throwing darts at balloons. By hitting the balloons they could earn either nine points, six points, or two points. Judy won the top prize by scoring 34 points. What is the least number of darts that Judy could have thrown to get exactly 34 points? (What other possibilities are there?)

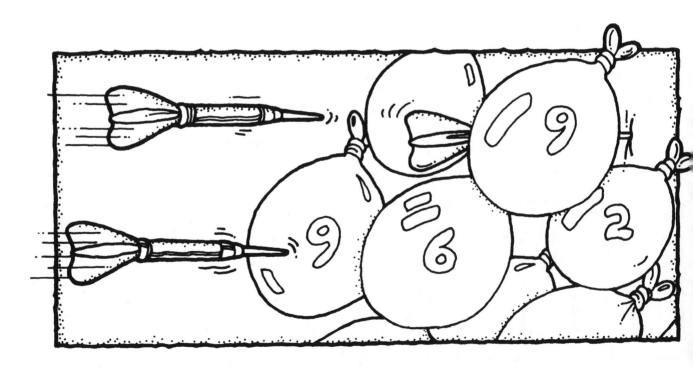

Task Completion

Tangram shapes can be combined in many interesting ways to make people, animals, and things. Cut out the pieces and use them to make the shapes shown below. Have someone check your work before you work on the next shape.

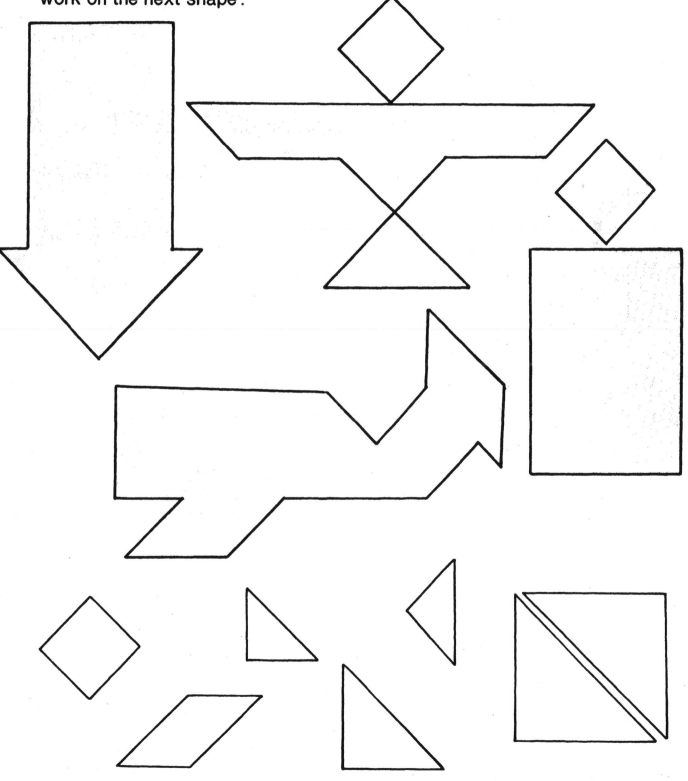

Fill in the squares with letters that will make real words. When you have filled in all of the blanks, try to add onto the puzzle by drawing squares of your own and filling them in with more words.

						S	O		
C	H	I	L	D	R	E	N		
		T		R		V			
						E			
						N			
	D	E	T	E	R	M	I	N	E

Answers

Finding Out
1. No
2. No, but they use high pitches like sonar to navigate at night.
3. To make it softer and easier to swallow because raccoons have small throats
4. No. They are color blind. They charge at the motion of the cape.
5. No
6. They swim with their mouths open in order to breathe.
7. No. The blue whale is the largest.

Animal Scramble
1. cat
2. horse
3. duck
4. donkey
5. giraffe
6. rabbit
7. goat
8. monkey
9. whale
10. turkey
11. shark
12. dolphin
13. armadillo
14. elephant
15. rhinoceros
16. hippopotamus

Vocabulary
Some possible answers are:

S – R star, stir, sir, sour, spear, soar, scour

P – L pull, pill, pal, pool, pail, peel, pencil

B – K book, bank, black, beak, blank, break, brook

C – E case, close, chase, choose, cheese, clue, core

B – Y boy, buy, baby, bunny, busy, bay, berry

S – N sun, soon, seen, spin, spoon, screen, sin

T – N tin, tan, ton, then, than, thin, town

F – T foot, feet, fit, fort, first, frost, fist

Problem Solving
1. Making a chart is the best way to solve the first puzzle. Possible answers include 7 Moozos and 1 Ooglie, 4 Moozos and 5 Ooglies, 1 Moozo and 9 Ooglies.
2. The largest scores will produce the least number of darts. The least number that Judy could have thrown would be six (two 9's, two 6's and two 2's).

Task Completion

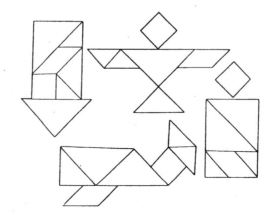

Printed in the United States
by Baker & Taylor Publisher Services